Little Frog was moving to a new lily pad.

"I will miss you," he said to Birdie. "How will I make new friends when I move?"

"Take my lucky feather,"
said Birdie. "It will help
you to make new friends."

Little Frog felt lonely
when he got to his new pad.
Then he saw a turtle
swim by.

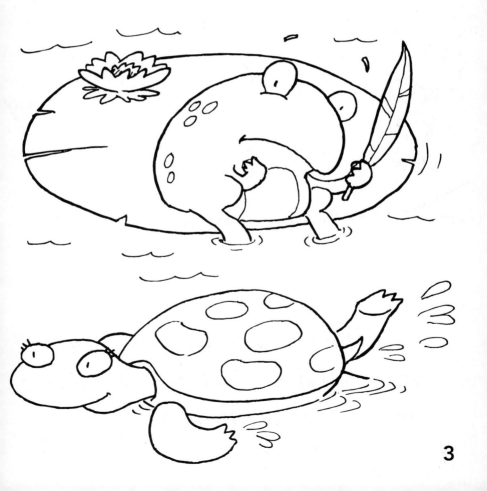

Little Frog squeezed his lucky feather and asked, "Turtle, will you be my friend?"

"Okay," said Turtle. "Hop in, and let's swim!"

While Little Frog swam,
he lost his feather.

Little Frog was sad.

"What's wrong?" asked Turtle.

Little Frog cried, "I can't find my lucky feather anywhere! Now you won't want to be my friend."

"You don't need a lucky
feather to be my friend!"
said Turtle.

Little Frog was happy.
He liked his new pad and
his new friend.